Table of Contents

I0410215

Introduction

In the ever-evolving landscape of technology, the role of engineering leaders has become paramount. As organizations strive to innovate, adapt, and excel in an increasingly competitive world, the demand for exceptional engineering leadership has never been greater. This book sets out to explore the intricate art of leading engineering teams, fostering innovation, and navigating the challenges of the modern tech industry.

In this age of rapid technological advancements, the role of an engineering leader extends far beyond technical expertise. Engineering leaders must be adept at aligning technical excellence with strategic goals, empowering teams to create impactful solutions, and cultivating a culture of collaboration and continuous learning. They are the compass that guides their teams through the complexities of projects, helping them navigate the unknown waters of uncertainty and change.

Drawing from the experiences of seasoned engineering leaders, this book delves into the multifaceted nature of leadership in technology-driven environments. It provides insights, strategies, and real-world examples that illuminate the path toward effective leadership in engineering disciplines. Whether you're a seasoned engineering manager seeking fresh perspectives or a budding technical professional aspiring to lead, this book offers practical guidance to help you chart your course to success.

Through a comprehensive exploration of topics such as communication, team dynamics, innovation, organizational strategy, and personal growth, this book equips readers with the tools they need to become not just proficient engineers, but inspirational leaders. As we embark on this journey through the intricacies of engineering leadership, we invite you to join us in discovering how to not only survive but thrive in the ever-changing world of technology.

So, fasten your seatbelt and prepare for a transformative expedition. Let's embark on this odyssey together, and uncover the principles and practices that will elevate your engineering leadership to new heights.

Why is it so difficult to find high quality engineering leadership?

Finding high-quality engineering leadership can be challenging for several reasons, as it requires a combination of technical expertise, leadership skills, and the ability to navigate complex organizational dynamics. Here are some factors that contribute to the difficulty of finding exceptional engineering leaders:

1. **Skill Set Combination**: Effective engineering leaders need a blend of technical proficiency and strong leadership skills. This combination is not always easy to find, as individuals with both attributes are relatively rare.
2. **Shortage of Experienced Leaders**: The demand for experienced engineering leaders often exceeds the supply, leading to competition for a limited pool of qualified candidates.
3. **Evolution of Technology**: The rapid pace of technological change requires leaders to stay up-to-date with the latest trends and tools, making it challenging to find candidates who are both technically adept and knowledgeable.
4. **Leadership vs. Individual Contributor**: Not all skilled engineers are interested in transitioning to leadership roles. Many prefer to remain in technical or individual contributor roles, leading to a smaller pool of potential leaders.
5. **Promotion from Within**: Organizations often promote engineers to leadership roles based on technical skills alone. While this can work, it doesn't always guarantee strong leadership abilities.
6. **Effective Communication Skills**: Engineering leaders must communicate with diverse stakeholders, including technical

and non-technical teams. Strong communication skills are critical but can be challenging to find.

7. **Complex Organizational Dynamics**: Engineering leadership involves navigating organizational politics, managing budgets, collaborating with other departments, and aligning with business goals.

8. **Multifaceted Responsibilities**: Engineering leaders are responsible for technical excellence, team motivation, project management, and strategic alignment—all of which require different skill sets.

9. **Retaining Technical Focus**: Transitioning to a leadership role can mean less time spent on hands-on technical work. Some engineers may be hesitant to give up their technical contributions.

10. **Cultural Fit**: An engineering leader needs to align with the organization's culture and values, which can be difficult to assess during the hiring process.

11. **Lack of Clear Pathways**: Many engineers may not see a clear career path for growth and development as engineering leaders, which can discourage them from pursuing leadership roles.

12. **High Expectations**: Engineering leaders are expected to deliver results, manage teams, and handle challenges effectively. Meeting these high expectations can be daunting.

13. **Interpersonal Skills**: Effective leadership requires building relationships, resolving conflicts, and motivating teams. Finding leaders with strong interpersonal skills can be challenging.

14. **Diverse Industries**: Engineering leadership roles exist in a variety of industries, each with its unique challenges and requirements, making it difficult to find leaders who can adapt across different domains.

What can an organization do to find more good leaders

To address the challenge of finding high-quality engineering leadership, organizations can take proactive steps, such as:

- Investing in leadership development programs to groom internal talent.
- Providing mentorship and coaching for engineers interested in transitioning to leadership roles.
- Broadening the search criteria to include candidates with potential and willingness to learn leadership skills.
- Offering clear growth paths and incentives for engineers to consider leadership roles.
- Focusing on both technical and soft skills during the hiring process.
- Promoting a culture that values leadership and offers opportunities for professional growth.

Overall, finding high-quality engineering leadership requires a holistic approach that considers both technical expertise and leadership qualities, along with a commitment to ongoing development and cultivation of leadership talent.

What are the general qualities of a good engineering leader

A good engineering leader possesses a combination of technical expertise, leadership skills, and a deep understanding of how to guide and support their team effectively. Here are some key qualities and attributes that make a good engineering leader:

- **Technical Proficiency**: An effective engineering leader should have a strong technical background and expertise in the field. This allows them to understand the challenges their team faces, make informed decisions, and provide technical guidance.
- **Communication Skills**: Clear and open communication is crucial for an engineering leader to convey expectations, share information, provide feedback, and foster collaboration within the team and with stakeholders.
- **Vision and Strategy**: A good leader sets a clear vision for the team's goals and aligns their efforts with the organization's strategic objectives. They can create a roadmap for achieving long-term success.
- **Empathy and Emotional Intelligence**: Understanding and relating to team members' experiences, concerns, and motivations helps create a positive and supportive work environment.
- **Problem-Solving Abilities**: Leaders need to be adept at analyzing complex situations, identifying problems, and devising effective solutions. They should encourage their team to tackle challenges creatively.
- **Adaptability**: The technology landscape is constantly changing. A good leader adapts to new trends, tools, and methodologies to keep the team relevant and competitive.

- **Delegation and Trust**: Effective leaders trust their team members to carry out tasks and make decisions independently. Delegating responsibilities demonstrates trust and empowers team members.
- **Motivational Skills**: Inspiring and motivating the team to achieve their best work is essential. Recognizing and celebrating achievements fosters a positive team culture.
- **Conflict Resolution**: Handling conflicts and disagreements professionally and respectfully is crucial. A leader who can mediate and find resolutions contributes to a harmonious team environment.
- **Coaching and Mentorship**: A great leader invests time in mentoring and developing team members. This fosters growth, enhances skills, and builds a strong team.
- **Decision-Making Abilities**: Leaders need to make tough decisions under pressure. Being able to make informed and timely decisions is a key leadership trait.
- **Ethical Integrity**: Leading with honesty, transparency, and ethical behavior builds trust with the team and stakeholders. It sets a positive example for others to follow.
- **Resilience**: The tech industry can be challenging, with setbacks and failures. A resilient leader maintains a positive attitude and guides the team through difficult times.
- **Collaboration**: Collaboration across teams is often necessary. A leader who fosters collaboration and breaks down silos can help achieve cross-functional success.
- **Continuous Learning**: A good engineering leader is always eager to learn and improve. Staying up-to-date with industry trends and seeking personal growth sets a positive example for the team.
- **Results-Oriented**: Ultimately, a leader is responsible for delivering results. Balancing technical excellence with achieving business goals is crucial for success.

- **Strategic Thinking**: A leader who can see the big picture and align technical decisions with broader business objectives can lead their team to meaningful contributions.
- **Feedback and Improvement**: Leaders should be receptive to feedback, both giving and receiving it. Continuously improving their own leadership skills contributes to team growth.

Overall, a good engineering leader combines technical acumen, interpersonal skills, and a clear vision to create an environment where their team can thrive, innovate, and achieve their full potential.

Why are so many engineers adverse to management or leadership roles?

Many engineers are adverse to management or leadership roles for a variety of reasons. While some engineers do eventually pursue management roles, many others prefer to remain in technical or individual contributor positions. Here are some common reasons why engineers might be hesitant to take on management or leadership roles:

- **Technical Passion**: Many engineers are deeply passionate about their technical work and enjoy the challenges of coding, problem-solving, and technical innovation. They may fear that transitioning to a leadership role could distance them from hands-on technical work.
- **Lack of Interest**: Some engineers simply have no interest in management or leadership responsibilities. They are content with their technical contributions and do not want the added responsibilities of managing people, projects, and budgets.
- **Different Skill Set**: Management and leadership roles require a different skill set than technical roles. Effective leadership demands skills in communication, conflict resolution, delegation, and strategic thinking—areas that some engineers might not feel comfortable or interested in developing.
- **Limited Exposure**: Engineers often have limited exposure to management and leadership during their education and early career. This lack of exposure can lead to misconceptions or uncertainties about what these roles entail.

- **Fear of Losing Technical Proficiency**: Engineers might worry that transitioning to a leadership role will cause them to lose touch with the latest technologies, tools, and coding practices, making it harder to provide effective guidance to their team.
- **Work-Life Balance**: Management roles can sometimes come with longer hours and increased stress, which can deter engineers who value work-life balance and the flexibility of technical roles.
- **Risk and Responsibility**: Leadership roles involve making critical decisions that can impact the success of projects and teams. Some engineers might be reluctant to take on this level of responsibility and the associated risks.
- **Organizational Politics**: Some engineers perceive management roles as being more involved in organizational politics and bureaucracy, which might not align with their values or interests.
- **Recognition and Status**: Engineers can achieve recognition and status through their technical accomplishments. Transitioning to a leadership role might not offer the same level of recognition or satisfaction.
- **Staying Current**: The technology landscape evolves rapidly, and engineers might be concerned about their ability to stay current with the latest trends and developments while also fulfilling leadership responsibilities.
- **Personal Preference**: Some engineers are naturally introverted or prefer to work independently, which might make them less inclined to take on leadership roles that require extensive interaction with others.
- **Training and Development**: Many engineering programs focus on technical skills, but there is often less emphasis on leadership development. Engineers might lack the training

and resources to effectively transition into leadership positions.

It's important to recognize that not all engineers shy away from management or leadership roles, and some find the transition to be fulfilling and rewarding. Organizations can help address these concerns by providing clear career paths, offering leadership training, and allowing engineers to pursue growth in both technical and leadership aspects of their careers. Ultimately, a diverse mix of technical and leadership roles contributes to a well-rounded and successful engineering organization.

Technical Proficiency

Technical proficiency is critically important for an engineering leader for several reasons. While leadership skills are essential for guiding and managing teams, having a solid technical foundation enables leaders to effectively understand, communicate, and make informed decisions about complex technical matters. Here's why technical proficiency matters for an engineering leader:

- **Earns Respect**: Technical expertise commands respect from team members. When a leader demonstrates a deep understanding of the technology and can engage in meaningful technical discussions, team members are more likely to trust and follow their guidance.
- **Informed Decision-Making**: Technical leaders can make well-informed decisions regarding project direction, technical strategies, and solutions. They can assess the implications of different choices and make decisions that align with the team's capabilities and goals.
- **Effective Problem-Solving**: Technical leaders can actively contribute to problem-solving discussions, helping the team overcome technical challenges and providing creative solutions based on their experience and knowledge.
- **Empowerment**: A leader who understands the technical aspects of a project can empower team members by offering guidance, removing obstacles, and providing the necessary resources to ensure project success.
- **Collaboration and Communication**: Technical proficiency enables leaders to effectively communicate with both technical and non-technical stakeholders. Clear communication is crucial for aligning goals, expectations, and project progress.

- **Mentoring and Coaching**: A technically skilled leader can provide valuable mentorship and coaching to team members, helping them develop their technical skills and career paths.
- **Foster Innovation**: Leaders who are knowledgeable about emerging technologies and trends can drive innovation within the team. They can identify opportunities for implementing new tools, techniques, and practices.
- **Quality Assurance**: Technical leaders understand the importance of code quality, testing, and best practices. They can ensure that the team adheres to high standards and produces reliable, maintainable software.
- **Effective Feedback**: Providing constructive feedback becomes more meaningful when it comes from someone who understands the technical intricacies of the work. Technical leaders can give specific, actionable feedback that helps team members improve.
- **Technical Roadmapping**: Leaders with technical proficiency can create effective technical roadmaps that align with business goals and the team's capabilities. They can set a clear vision for the technical direction of the project.
- **Critical Evaluation**: Technical leaders can critically assess the feasibility and viability of proposed solutions. They can identify potential risks, challenges, and trade-offs that might not be apparent to those without a technical background.
- **Resolving Technical Disputes**: When disagreements arise about technical decisions, a technically skilled leader can mediate and provide an informed perspective that helps the team reach consensus.
- **Lead by Example**: Demonstrating technical excellence sets a positive example for the team. When leaders actively engage in technical work, it encourages team members to follow suit.

- **Maintain Credibility**: In a technical environment, leaders who can't contribute meaningfully to technical discussions might lose credibility and struggle to inspire confidence in their decisions.

Balancing technical proficiency with leadership skills creates a well-rounded engineering leader who can effectively navigate both technical challenges and team dynamics. Technical leaders who can guide their teams with confidence, provide direction, and understand the intricacies of their work contribute to the success of projects and the growth of their team members.

Communication Skills

Communication skills are crucial for engineering leaders because they facilitate effective collaboration, alignment, and decision-making within engineering teams and across the organization. An engineering leader's ability to communicate clearly, empathetically, and strategically has a significant impact on the success of projects, team morale, and overall organizational outcomes. Here's why communication skills are important for an engineering leader:

- **Clear Communication**: Effective communication ensures that expectations, goals, and project requirements are clearly understood by team members. Miscommunication can lead to misunderstandings, errors, and delays.
- **Alignment**: Communication helps align the team's efforts with the organization's goals and strategic vision. A leader who can articulate the "why" behind decisions and initiatives fosters a sense of purpose among team members.
- **Stakeholder Engagement**: Engineering leaders often interact with various stakeholders, including executives, product managers, and customers. Strong communication skills enable leaders to convey technical information to non-technical stakeholders and build relationships.
- **Team Building**: Clear communication fosters a positive team culture by encouraging open discussions, active listening, and mutual respect. This creates a supportive and collaborative environment where team members feel comfortable sharing ideas and concerns.
- **Feedback and Recognition**: Providing constructive feedback and recognizing team members' contributions are essential for growth and motivation. Effective communication helps leaders give feedback that is actionable, specific, and respectful.

- **Conflict Resolution**: Conflicts and disagreements are inevitable in any team. An engineering leader with strong communication skills can mediate conflicts, address concerns, and find resolutions that promote harmony.
- **Motivation and Inspiration**: Leaders who can communicate a compelling vision and inspire their team create a sense of purpose and commitment. Effective communication rallies the team around common goals.
- **Decision-Making**: Leaders often make decisions based on a range of information. Clear communication ensures that team members understand the rationale behind decisions, which fosters trust and buy-in.
- **Problem-Solving**: Communication is essential for identifying and solving technical challenges. Leaders who can communicate complex problems and solutions effectively drive efficient problem-solving processes.
- **Adaptability**: The ability to adapt communication style to different audiences — whether technical or non-technical — is essential for successful collaboration and conveying information accurately.
- **Change Management**: When changes occur in projects or processes, effective communication helps the team understand the reasons for the change and manage the transition smoothly.
- **Technical Documentation**: Communicating technical concepts through documentation, diagrams, and presentations ensures that knowledge is shared and preserved for the team's benefit.
- **Visibility and Transparency**: Sharing project status, progress, and challenges with stakeholders promotes transparency and enables informed decision-making.

- **Crisis Management**: During critical situations, leaders need to communicate clearly, calmly, and with authority to guide the team through challenges.
- **Professional Growth**: Leaders who can communicate growth opportunities and development plans to team members contribute to individual and collective growth.
- **Networking and Collaboration**: Strong communication skills enable leaders to build professional networks, collaborate with other teams, and stay informed about industry trends.

Effective communication skills empower engineering leaders to bridge the gap between technical expertise and organizational success. Leaders who can communicate with clarity, empathy, and purpose create a positive team environment, enhance productivity, and drive meaningful outcomes.

Vision and Strategy

Vision and strategy skills are essential for engineering leaders as they provide a roadmap for the team's direction, align efforts with organizational goals, and guide decision-making. An engineering leader's ability to develop a clear vision and implement effective strategies can significantly impact the success of projects, team morale, and the organization's overall competitiveness. Here's why vision and strategy skills are important for an engineering leader:

- **Alignment with Organizational Goals**: A strong vision helps engineering teams understand how their work contributes to the organization's larger objectives. Leaders who align their team's efforts with the company's strategic goals create a sense of purpose and direction.
- **Inspiration and Motivation**: A compelling vision inspires team members by showing them the potential impact of their work. It motivates them to go above and beyond their tasks and invest in the team's success.
- **Clear Direction**: A well-defined vision provides clarity on the team's mission, priorities, and long-term goals. It helps team members make decisions that are consistent with the larger strategic direction.
- **Innovation**: A visionary leader encourages innovative thinking and exploration of new ideas. By fostering a culture of innovation, leaders can drive the team to explore novel solutions and technologies.
- **Adaptability**: In a rapidly changing technological landscape, a leader's ability to adapt the team's vision and strategies enables the team to respond to new opportunities and challenges effectively.
- **Resource Allocation**: Strategic thinking helps leaders allocate resources, such as time, budget, and talent, to

projects that align with the team's goals and deliver the most value to the organization.

- **Risk Management**: Visionary leaders anticipate potential risks and challenges. Developing strategies to mitigate risks ensures smoother project execution and minimizes disruptions.
- **Long-Term Planning**: Visionary leaders think beyond immediate tasks and plan for the team's long-term growth, development, and success.
- **Talent Development**: A strategic leader identifies team members' strengths and areas for growth. They create development plans that align with the team's vision and the organization's needs.
- **Change Management**: When organizational changes occur, leaders with strong vision and strategy skills can guide the team through transitions while maintaining focus on the long-term goals.
- **Communication and Alignment**: A well-communicated vision fosters alignment among team members, ensuring that everyone understands and works toward the same goals.
- **Customer-Centric Approach**: A clear vision helps leaders prioritize customer needs and develop strategies to deliver products that meet those needs.
- **Decision-Making**: A strategic leader can make informed decisions that align with the team's vision and objectives. This ensures that decisions contribute to the team's overall success.
- **Competitive Advantage**: Visionary leaders develop strategies that position the team to outperform competitors and seize opportunities in the market.

- **Cultural Impact**: Leaders who communicate a compelling vision can shape the team's culture and values, fostering a positive and collaborative work environment.
- **Measurable Outcomes**: Effective strategies set specific goals and metrics, enabling leaders to measure progress and track the team's performance over time.

Vision and strategy skills empower engineering leaders to guide their teams with purpose, direction, and long-term goals. Leaders who can create and communicate a clear vision while developing strategies to achieve it enable their teams to achieve meaningful results, innovate, and contribute to the organization's success.

Empathy and Emotional Intelligence

Empathy and emotional intelligence are indispensable qualities for engineering leaders as they drive effective collaboration, build strong relationships, and foster a positive work environment. Engineering leaders who possess these qualities are better equipped to understand and support their team members, navigate challenges, and lead with authenticity. Here's why empathy and emotional intelligence are crucial for an engineering leader:

- **Building Trust**: Empathy and emotional intelligence create a foundation of trust within the team. When team members feel understood and valued, they are more likely to trust their leader's decisions and guidance.
- **Effective Communication**: Leaders with emotional intelligence can communicate with sensitivity and clarity. They consider the emotional impact of their words and tailor their communication style to resonate with their team.
- **Active Listening**: Empathetic leaders are skilled listeners who actively engage with their team members. They listen not only to the words being said but also to the underlying emotions and concerns.
- **Conflict Resolution**: Emotional intelligence helps leaders navigate conflicts and disagreements with grace and empathy. They can mediate disputes, address concerns, and find solutions that respect everyone's perspective.
- **Motivation and Morale**: Leaders who understand their team members' motivations and emotions can provide the right kind of support and encouragement, boosting team morale and motivation.

- **Adaptability**: Leaders with emotional intelligence can adapt their leadership style to the needs and preferences of individual team members, creating a more personalized and effective approach.
- *Empowering Team Members*: Empathetic leaders empower their team members by acknowledging their strengths, providing autonomy, and creating opportunities for growth.
- **Reducing Stress**: Leaders who recognize and manage their own emotions effectively can set a positive tone for the team. This helps reduce stress and create a healthier work environment.
- **Cultivating Collaboration**: Emotional intelligence enhances collaboration by fostering an atmosphere of respect and open communication, allowing team members to work together more effectively.
- **Mentorship and Development**: Empathetic leaders understand their team members' career aspirations and can provide guidance, mentorship, and development opportunities tailored to individual needs.
- **Handling Feedback**: Leaders who can give and receive feedback with empathy create an environment where feedback is seen as constructive and beneficial rather than critical.
- **Crisis Management**: During challenging situations, leaders with emotional intelligence can remain composed and provide support to their team, helping them navigate uncertainty and adversity.
- **Retention and Engagement**: An empathetic leader understands what motivates team members and can create an environment where they feel valued and engaged, reducing turnover.

- **Inclusivity**: Leaders with empathy and emotional intelligence create an inclusive environment where diverse perspectives are respected and valued.
- **Lead by Example**: Modeling emotional intelligence encourages team members to also practice empathy and emotional awareness in their interactions.
- **Ethical Decision-Making**: Leaders who consider the ethical and moral implications of their decisions contribute to a culture of integrity and ethical behavior.

Empathy and emotional intelligence enable engineering leaders to lead with understanding, compassion, and authenticity. These qualities foster a positive team culture, enhance collaboration, and enable leaders to connect with their team members on a deeper level. By prioritizing empathy and emotional intelligence, engineering leaders can create an environment where team members feel supported, motivated, and empowered to achieve their best work.

Problem-Solving Abilities

Problem-solving abilities are a critical trait for engineering leaders, as they enable leaders to navigate complex challenges, make informed decisions, and guide their teams toward effective solutions. Engineering leaders who excel in problem-solving contribute to the success of projects, the growth of their teams, and the overall success of the organization. Here's why problem-solving abilities are important for an engineering leader:

- **Navigating Technical Challenges**: Engineering projects often involve technical complexities and obstacles. A leader with strong problem-solving skills can guide the team in overcoming these challenges by analyzing the situation, identifying root causes, and devising practical solutions.
- **Informed Decision-Making**: Problem-solving skills enable leaders to make informed decisions that are grounded in data, analysis, and critical thinking. This leads to more effective and strategic choices for the team.
- **Critical Thinking**: Engineering leaders need to assess situations from multiple angles, considering different perspectives and potential outcomes. Effective problem-solving requires strong critical thinking skills.
- **Conflict Resolution**: Conflicts and disagreements are common in any team. Leaders who are adept at problem-solving can mediate conflicts, address underlying issues, and find resolutions that satisfy all parties involved.
- **Innovation and Creativity**: Problem-solving skills foster innovation by encouraging leaders to think outside the box and explore new approaches. Leaders who embrace creative problem-solving inspire their teams to innovate as well.
- **Risk Management**: Identifying potential risks and developing strategies to mitigate them is crucial for

successful project execution. Problem-solving abilities help leaders anticipate challenges and plan for contingencies.

- **Effective Resource Utilization**: Problem-solving skills help leaders allocate resources — such as time, budget, and manpower — effectively. This ensures that resources are used efficiently to achieve optimal results.
- **Adaptability**: The ability to adapt and pivot in response to unexpected challenges is important for any leader. Problem-solving skills enable leaders to adjust their strategies and tactics as needed.
- **Team Development**: Guiding the team through problem-solving processes can help develop team members' critical thinking and analytical skills, contributing to their professional growth.
- **Root Cause Analysis**: Effective problem-solving involves identifying the underlying causes of issues rather than just addressing surface-level symptoms. This leads to more sustainable solutions.
- **Confidence and Trust**: A leader who can analyze problems, propose solutions, and guide the team toward successful outcomes builds confidence and trust among team members and stakeholders.
- **Complex Project Management**: Many engineering projects involve complex systems and interconnected components. Problem-solving skills help leaders manage and integrate these complexities effectively.
- **Communication**: Leaders who can communicate problem-solving approaches clearly and transparently help the team understand the rationale behind decisions and solutions.
- **Continuous Improvement**: Problem-solving skills contribute to a culture of continuous improvement, where teams learn from challenges and iteratively enhance their processes.

- **Stakeholder Satisfaction**: Effective problem-solving leads to better outcomes for customers, clients, and stakeholders, enhancing their satisfaction with the team's work.
- **Time Management**: Problem-solving skills enable leaders to prioritize tasks, allocate time effectively, and optimize work processes.

Strong problem-solving abilities empower engineering leaders to overcome challenges, make well-informed decisions, and guide their teams toward success. Leaders who excel in problem-solving foster innovation, resilience, and effective decision-making, contributing to the overall growth and effectiveness of their teams and organizations.

Adaptability

Adaptability is a crucial trait for engineering leaders because it enables them to thrive in dynamic environments, navigate change, and lead their teams effectively through uncertainty. An engineering leader's ability to adapt to evolving circumstances, technologies, and challenges is essential for maintaining productivity, fostering innovation, and achieving long-term success. Here's why adaptability is important for an engineering leader:

- **Navigating Change**: Engineering projects often encounter changes in requirements, technologies, and market conditions. An adaptable leader can guide the team through these changes, ensuring that projects remain on track and aligned with goals.
- **Evolving Technologies**: The tech industry is characterized by rapid technological advancements. Leaders who can adapt to new tools, frameworks, and methodologies stay relevant and lead their teams in adopting innovative solutions.
- **Resilience in Uncertainty**: Adaptable leaders can maintain composure and lead with confidence during uncertain times, reassuring the team and keeping them focused on the task at hand.
- **Flexibility in Methods**: Adaptable leaders understand that there's no one-size-fits-all approach to problem-solving. They're open to trying different methods and approaches to find the best solution for a given situation.
- **Change Management**: When organizational changes occur, adaptable leaders can communicate the rationale behind changes, address concerns, and guide the team through transitions.

- **Crisis Management**: During crises or unexpected events, an adaptable leader can quickly assess the situation, make informed decisions, and guide the team toward effective solutions.
- **Cross-Functional Collaboration**: Engineering leaders often collaborate with teams from different departments. Adaptability helps them understand diverse perspectives and find common ground.
- **Agility in Problem-Solving**: Adaptable leaders can assess problems from multiple angles and tailor their approach to fit the context, leading to more effective and tailored solutions.

Adaptability is a critical skill that empowers engineering leaders to navigate change, lead with resilience, and guide their teams toward success in the face of evolving challenges. Leaders who embrace adaptability foster innovation, inspire growth, and contribute to a culture of continuous improvement within their teams and organizations.

Delegation and Trust

Delegation and trust are fundamental skills for engineering leaders as they empower teams, promote efficiency, and foster a culture of collaboration. Leaders who can effectively delegate tasks and trust their team members contribute to higher productivity, professional growth, and successful project outcomes. Here's why delegation and trust are important for an engineering leader:

- **Effective Resource Management**: Delegation allows leaders to distribute tasks based on team members' strengths, skills, and availability. This ensures that resources are utilized optimally and that tasks are assigned to those best suited to handle them.
- **Time Management**: Leaders can focus on high-level strategic decisions and responsibilities by delegating tasks that can be handled by other team members. This leads to better time allocation and improved productivity.
- **Skill Development**: Delegation provides team members with opportunities to learn and develop new skills. Leaders who delegate effectively contribute to the growth and advancement of their team members.
- **Empowerment and Ownership**: Delegation empowers team members to take ownership of their work. When individuals have autonomy and responsibility, they are more engaged and motivated to excel.
- **Team Morale**: Trusting team members with important tasks boosts their confidence and morale. It demonstrates that leaders value their contributions and believe in their capabilities.
- **Collaboration**: Effective delegation promotes collaboration as team members work together to accomplish tasks. It

encourages knowledge sharing and cross-functional cooperation.

- **Efficiency and Scalability**: Delegation allows leaders to scale their efforts by leveraging the skills and capabilities of the entire team. This leads to greater efficiency and the ability to handle larger workloads.
- **Decision-Making Distribution**: Leaders can distribute decision-making responsibilities by delegating authority to team members. This prevents bottlenecks and empowers team members to make informed decisions.
- **Risk Management**: Delegating tasks to team members who possess the required expertise reduces the risk of errors and improves the quality of work.
- **Focus on Strategy**: Leaders can focus on strategic planning, innovation, and long-term vision when routine tasks are delegated to capable team members.
- **Personal Growth**: Delegation encourages leaders to step back from micro-management and allows them to grow by focusing on higher-level leadership skills.
- **Time for Innovation**: Leaders who delegate effectively have more time to dedicate to innovative projects and exploring new opportunities for the team.
- **Feedback and Improvement**: Delegating tasks creates opportunities for feedback and improvement. Leaders can provide guidance and mentorship to team members, helping them refine their skills.
- **Trust-Building**: Delegating tasks demonstrates trust in team members' abilities. This builds a culture of mutual trust and respect within the team.
- **Conflict Resolution**: Delegating tasks that involve resolving conflicts or addressing challenges can lead to diverse perspectives and creative solutions.

- **Reduced Burnout**: Effective delegation prevents leaders from becoming overwhelmed by their responsibilities, reducing the risk of burnout.

Delegation and trust are vital skills for engineering leaders that contribute to team development, efficiency, and overall success. Leaders who delegate wisely and trust their team members foster an environment of empowerment, collaboration, and continuous growth, resulting in improved project outcomes and a positive team culture.

Motivational Skills

Motivation skills are essential for engineering leaders as they influence team morale, engagement, and performance. Leaders who can effectively motivate their team members create a positive work environment, foster commitment, and drive productivity. Here's why motivation skills are important for an engineering leader:

- **Higher Productivity**: Motivated team members are more productive and committed to their work. Engineering leaders who can inspire and energize their teams drive higher levels of performance and output.
- **Employee Engagement**: Motivation skills increase employee engagement by creating a sense of purpose and alignment with the team's goals. Engaged team members are more likely to contribute their best efforts and stay invested in the team's success.
- **Positive Work Environment**: Leaders who prioritize motivation contribute to a positive and supportive work environment. This encourages collaboration, teamwork, and open communication.
- **Employee Satisfaction**: Motivated team members are generally more satisfied with their work. Satisfied employees are likely to stay with the organization, reducing turnover and associated costs.
- **Creativity and Innovation**: Motivated teams are more likely to think creatively and generate innovative solutions. Leaders who foster motivation encourage team members to explore new ideas and approaches.
- **Goal Achievement**: Motivation skills help team members stay focused on achieving their goals. Leaders who keep the team motivated ensure that projects are completed successfully and on time.

- **Adaptability**: Motivated team members are more willing to embrace change and adapt to new challenges. Leaders who foster motivation facilitate smoother transitions during times of change.
- **Continuous Improvement**: Leaders who prioritize motivation encourage a culture of continuous improvement. Team members are motivated to seek ways to enhance processes and outcomes.
- **Effective Communication**: Motivated teams communicate more openly and constructively. Leaders who motivate their teams create an environment where ideas and feedback flow freely.
- **Resilience**: Motivated team members are better equipped to handle setbacks and challenges. Leaders who inspire motivation help their teams bounce back from adversity more effectively.
- **Team Morale**: Leaders who can motivate their teams contribute to higher morale, leading to increased job satisfaction and a positive atmosphere.
- **Personal Growth**: Motivation skills support team members' personal and professional growth. Leaders who inspire motivation encourage skill development and career advancement.
- **Recognition and Rewards**: Motivated teams are more likely to appreciate and respond positively to recognition and rewards. Leaders who motivate their teams ensure that efforts are acknowledged and celebrated.
- **Conflict Resolution**: Motivated team members are more likely to approach conflicts with a positive mindset and seek productive resolutions.
- **Empowerment**: Motivated teams feel empowered to take ownership of their work and contribute to the team's

success. Leaders who foster motivation empower team members to make decisions and take initiative.

- **Long-Term Success**: Leaders who prioritize motivation contribute to the team's long-term success by fostering a culture of commitment, dedication, and enthusiasm.

Motivation skills are a key factor in driving the success of engineering teams. Leaders who can inspire and maintain motivation create an environment where team members thrive, collaborate, and achieve their best work. By fostering motivation, engineering leaders contribute to the overall growth, performance, and success of their teams and organizations.

Conflict Resolution

Conflict resolution skills are crucial for engineering leaders as they enable effective collaboration, maintain team cohesion, and ensure a healthy work environment. Leaders who can address conflicts constructively contribute to improved communication, productivity, and overall team performance. Here's why conflict resolution skills are important for an engineering leader:

- **Maintaining Productivity**: Conflicts can disrupt workflows and hinder progress. Leaders who can resolve conflicts quickly and effectively ensure that projects stay on track and deadlines are met.
- **Team Cohesion**: Conflict resolution helps prevent divisions within the team. Leaders who address conflicts promptly promote unity and a sense of camaraderie among team members.
- **Communication Improvement**: Effective conflict resolution involves open and honest communication. Leaders who facilitate resolution create an environment where team members are encouraged to voice their concerns and opinions.
- **Problem-Solving**: Conflict resolution requires identifying the underlying issues and finding solutions. Leaders who can guide the team toward constructive solutions enhance problem-solving skills and teamwork.
- **Trust-Building**: Successfully resolving conflicts builds trust among team members and with the leader. Trust is vital for effective collaboration and a positive work environment.
- **Healthy Work Culture**: Leaders who prioritize conflict resolution foster a culture where differences are acknowledged and addressed constructively, promoting a respectful and inclusive work environment.

- **Effective Decision-Making**: Leaders who can mediate conflicts ensure that decisions are made collectively and with input from all parties involved, leading to better decisions and outcomes.
- **Reducing Stress**: Conflicts can create stress and tension among team members. Leaders who resolve conflicts alleviate this stress, contributing to a healthier work environment.
- **Innovation**: Conflict resolution encourages diverse perspectives and ideas. Leaders who address conflicts in a positive manner stimulate creativity and innovation within the team.
- **Retention and Engagement**: A healthy work environment with effective conflict resolution practices increases employee satisfaction and engagement, reducing turnover.
- **Personal Growth**: Developing conflict resolution skills helps leaders refine their interpersonal and communication skills, contributing to their own personal growth.
- **Role Modeling**: Leaders who handle conflicts with professionalism and respect set an example for team members, guiding them on how to handle disagreements constructively.
- **Cross-Functional Collaboration**: Conflicts can arise when collaborating with other teams or departments. Leaders who are adept at conflict resolution facilitate successful cross-functional partnerships.
- **Clear Communication**: Conflict resolution requires clear communication and active listening. Leaders who excel in resolving conflicts promote effective communication throughout the team.
- **Employee Well-Being**: Resolving conflicts contributes to a positive workplace culture that values employee well-being and mental health.

- **Mitigating Escalation**: Effective conflict resolution prevents minor disagreements from escalating into larger issues that can disrupt team dynamics and project progress.

Conflict resolution skills are essential for engineering leaders to maintain a harmonious work environment, promote effective teamwork, and foster open communication. Leaders who can address conflicts with empathy, respect, and skill contribute to a positive team culture, improved collaboration, and the overall success of their teams and projects.

Coaching and Mentorship

Coaching and mentorship are essential skills for engineering leaders as they contribute to the professional growth, skill development, and success of team members. Leaders who can effectively coach and mentor their team members create a supportive and empowering work environment, fostering continuous learning and improved performance. Here's why coaching and mentorship are important for an engineering leader:

- **Skill Development**: Coaching and mentorship help team members develop technical and soft skills necessary for their roles. Leaders who provide guidance facilitate skill enhancement and career growth.
- **Knowledge Transfer**: Experienced leaders can share their knowledge and expertise with less experienced team members, accelerating their learning curve and preventing knowledge silos.
- **Confidence Building**: Coaching and mentorship boost team members' confidence by providing guidance, feedback, and encouragement. Confident team members are more likely to take on challenges and excel in their roles.
- **Goal Alignment**: Leaders who provide coaching help team members set and achieve meaningful goals that align with both individual aspirations and the team's objectives.
- **Feedback Loop**: Coaching and mentorship involve ongoing feedback. Leaders who offer constructive feedback enable team members to improve their skills and performance continuously.
- **Career Development**: Effective coaching and mentorship support team members' career advancement. Leaders who

invest in their team members' growth enhance retention and contribute to succession planning.

- **Personalized Approach**: Coaching and mentorship allow leaders to tailor their guidance to each team member's unique needs and learning style, enhancing the impact of their support.
- **Problem-Solving Skills**: Leaders who act as mentors can guide team members through complex challenges, teaching them how to approach problems and develop effective solutions.
- **Cross-Functional Learning**: Coaching and mentorship can expose team members to different areas of expertise within the organization, fostering cross-functional learning and collaboration.
- **Leadership Development**: Coaching and mentorship offer leadership training to potential future leaders. Leaders who nurture leadership qualities in their team members contribute to the organization's succession planning.
- **Motivation and Engagement**: Coaching and mentorship demonstrate a leader's investment in team members' success, increasing their motivation and engagement in their work.
- **Positive Work Culture**: Leaders who provide coaching and mentorship foster a positive and supportive work culture where team members feel valued and encouraged to grow.
- **Knowledge Sharing**: Effective coaching and mentorship promote a culture of knowledge sharing and collaboration within the team.
- **Empowerment**: Coaching and mentorship empower team members to take ownership of their professional development and career trajectory.
- **Long-Term Success**: Leaders who provide coaching and mentorship contribute to the long-term success of their

teams by nurturing a skilled, motivated, and engaged workforce.

- **Leadership Legacy**: Effective coaches and mentors leave a positive legacy by shaping the next generation of engineering talent and leaders within the organization.

Coaching and mentorship are crucial skills for engineering leaders to guide their team members' growth, development, and success. Leaders who invest in coaching and mentorship contribute to a culture of continuous learning, professional advancement, and collaboration, leading to enhanced performance and a more capable and confident team.

Decision-Making Abilities

Decision-making abilities are a cornerstone of effective engineering leadership, shaping the trajectory of projects, teams, and organizations. In the dynamic world of engineering, leaders who possess strong decision-making skills serve as the compass that steers their teams through challenges, uncertainties, and opportunities. The significance of decision-making abilities for an engineering leader is multi-faceted and far-reaching:

- **Strategic Alignment**: Engineering leaders make decisions that align with the overarching goals and strategies of the organization. Their ability to understand the big picture ensures that every decision contributes to the long-term success of the project and the company.
- **Resource Optimization**: Decision-making skills empower leaders to allocate resources wisely. By weighing the needs of projects against available resources, leaders can optimize budgets, time, and manpower for maximum efficiency.
- **Risk Management**: Effective decision-makers assess risks comprehensively, enabling them to proactively identify potential obstacles and develop mitigation strategies. This skill minimizes disruptions and fosters a culture of preparedness.
- **Innovation Catalyst**: Leaders who make informed decisions encourage innovation by evaluating new technologies, approaches, and ideas. Their ability to embrace calculated risks paves the way for transformative solutions.
- **Team Empowerment**: Sound decision-making provides clarity to team members, empowering them to move forward confidently. Decisive leaders create an environment where individuals understand their roles and can contribute effectively.

- **Problem-Solving**: Decision-making prowess equips leaders to tackle complex problems with a systematic approach. Their ability to analyze situations, weigh options, and choose the best course of action leads to effective solutions.
- **Communication Proficiency**: Strong decision-makers communicate their choices transparently, ensuring that team members understand the rationale behind decisions. Clear communication cultivates trust and collaboration.
- **Adaptability**: Engineering landscapes are rife with change. Leaders who make informed decisions based on changing circumstances guide their teams through evolving challenges while maintaining stability.
- **Stakeholder Satisfaction**: Decision-making skills take into account the interests of various stakeholders—clients, users, and partners—ensuring that choices align with their expectations and needs.
- **Ethical Leadership**: Ethical decision-making upholds the integrity of engineering projects and the organization as a whole. Leaders who prioritize ethical considerations build a culture of trust and credibility.
- **Effective Leadership**: Strong decision-making enhances leadership credibility. The ability to make timely, informed decisions inspires confidence and followership among team members.
- **Personal Growth**: The process of decision-making fosters leaders' personal growth. Evaluating options, learning from outcomes, and refining approaches contribute to ongoing development.
- **Operational Excellence**: Leaders who make informed decisions enhance operational efficiency. By focusing resources on high-impact initiatives, they contribute to the organization's overall excellence.

- **Long-Term Impact**: Well-considered decisions have enduring effects. An engineering leader's choices can shape the trajectory of a project, impact the lives of end-users, and contribute to the organization's legacy.

Decision-making abilities are at the heart of effective engineering leadership. Leaders who possess this skill set wield the power to navigate complexities, drive innovation, and lead their teams to success. By embracing a thoughtful and informed approach to decision-making, engineering leaders position themselves as the catalysts of positive change and progress in the field.

Ethical Integrity

Decision-making abilities are vital for engineering leaders as they drive project outcomes, team performance, and organizational success. Effective decision-making enables leaders to navigate complexities, allocate resources wisely, and guide their teams toward achieving strategic goals. Here's why decision-making abilities are important for an engineering leader:

- **Project Success**: Decision-making directly impacts project outcomes. Leaders who make informed and timely decisions contribute to successful project completion and delivery.
- **Risk Management**: Effective decision-making involves assessing potential risks and taking measures to mitigate them. Leaders who can make calculated decisions minimize the impact of risks on project timelines and objectives.
- **Resource Allocation**: Decision-making skills help leaders allocate resources—such as time, budget, and manpower—effectively, optimizing project efficiency and delivery.
- **Strategic Alignment**: Leaders make decisions that align with the organization's strategic goals and vision. Decisions that align with the bigger picture contribute to the organization's long-term success.
- **Team Empowerment**: Leaders who make clear and well-informed decisions empower their team members by providing them with direction and clarity on their tasks and objectives.
- **Innovation and Creativity**: Decision-making can involve exploring innovative solutions and approaches. Leaders who make decisions that encourage creativity inspire their teams to think outside the box.
- **Conflict Resolution**: Decision-making skills are crucial for resolving conflicts and disagreements within the team.

Leaders who can make fair and impartial decisions promote team harmony and collaboration.

- **Adaptability**: Leaders who can make decisions quickly and adapt to changing circumstances help their teams navigate unexpected challenges and uncertainties.
- **Stakeholder Management**: Leaders make decisions that take into account the interests and expectations of various stakeholders, ensuring that projects align with their needs.
- **Accountability**: Effective decision-making holds leaders accountable for the consequences of their choices. Leaders who take responsibility for their decisions earn trust and respect from their teams.
- **Effective Communication**: Leaders who can explain their decision-making process and rationale clearly to their teams foster understanding and alignment.
- **Ethical Considerations**: Decision-making involves ethical considerations. Leaders who make ethically sound decisions contribute to a culture of integrity and ethical behavior within the team.
- **Customer-Centric Approach**: Leaders make decisions that prioritize customer needs and satisfaction. This leads to the development of products and solutions that meet customer expectations.
- **Prioritization**: Decision-making involves prioritizing tasks and objectives. Leaders who can effectively prioritize contribute to efficient project execution and time management.
- **Change Management**: Effective decision-making is essential during times of change or organizational transitions. Leaders who can make decisions that guide the team through changes create a sense of stability.
- **Continuous Improvement**: Leaders who make decisions that promote continuous improvement contribute to a

culture of learning, growth, and enhanced team performance.

Strong decision-making abilities are critical for engineering leaders to guide their teams, projects, and organizations toward success. Leaders who can make well-informed, strategic decisions contribute to effective resource utilization, risk management, and a culture of accountability and innovation. Effective decision-making enhances team performance, project outcomes, and the overall achievement of organizational objectives.

Resilience

Resilience is a crucial trait for engineering leaders as it enables them to navigate challenges, setbacks, and uncertainties with a positive and adaptable mindset. Resilient leaders can effectively manage stress, inspire their teams, and lead through change, contributing to the overall success of projects and the well-being of their team members. Here's why resilience is important for an engineering leader:

- Handling Adversity: Resilient leaders can bounce back from setbacks, setbacks, and failures. They demonstrate a willingness to learn from challenges and keep moving forward.
- Stress Management: Engineering projects can be demanding and stressful. Resilient leaders manage their stress levels effectively, preventing burnout and promoting a healthier work environment.
- Change Adaptation: Resilient leaders embrace change and guide their teams through transitions. They foster an environment where team members feel supported during periods of uncertainty.
- Optimism and Positivity: Resilient leaders maintain an optimistic outlook, even in the face of difficulties. This positive attitude can inspire and motivate team members.
- Problem-Solving: Resilience enhances problem-solving skills, allowing leaders to approach challenges with creativity and determination to find solutions.
- Decision-Making Under Pressure: Resilient leaders can make informed decisions even in high-pressure situations. Their ability to stay composed contributes to effective decision-making.

- Team Morale: Resilient leaders help maintain team morale during tough times. Their ability to stay positive and focused encourages team members to do the same.
- Leading by Example: Resilient leaders model the behavior they want to see in their teams. They set a standard for facing challenges head-on and staying determined.
- Conflict Resolution: Resilient leaders approach conflicts with composure and a problem-solving mindset. They can navigate disagreements constructively and find solutions.
- Learning and Growth: Resilience encourages continuous learning and personal growth. Leaders who embrace challenges as learning opportunities set an example for their team members.
- Change Catalyst: Resilient leaders drive change initiatives by showing that challenges can be overcome with the right approach and attitude.
- Communication in Crisis: Resilient leaders can communicate effectively during times of crisis, reassuring team members and stakeholders with clear and honest communication.
- Building Trust: Resilient leaders who handle challenges with integrity and transparency build trust among team members and stakeholders.
- Risk Management: Resilience allows leaders to navigate risks and uncertainties confidently, making informed decisions to mitigate potential negative outcomes.
- Crisis Leadership: Resilient leaders can lead their teams through crises by remaining composed, making tough decisions, and maintaining a sense of direction.
- Long-Term Success: Resilient leaders contribute to the long-term success of projects and organizations by steering their teams through challenges and uncertainties.

Resilience is a valuable trait that empowers engineering leaders to overcome obstacles, inspire their teams, and maintain a positive work environment. Leaders who demonstrate resilience can effectively manage stress, lead through change, and foster a culture of adaptability and determination within their teams, leading to improved project outcomes and team well-being.

Collaboration

Collaboration is a crucial skill for engineering leaders as it fosters effective teamwork, innovation, and the successful execution of projects. Leaders who prioritize collaboration create an environment where team members work together cohesively, share ideas, and leverage diverse expertise. Here's why collaboration is important for an engineering leader:

- **Cross-Functional Expertise**: Collaboration allows team members to combine their skills and expertise from various disciplines, leading to well-rounded solutions.
- **Innovation**: Collaboration encourages the exchange of ideas and perspectives, leading to creative and innovative problem-solving approaches.
- **Knowledge Sharing**: Leaders who promote collaboration facilitate the sharing of knowledge and best practices among team members, enhancing the team's collective intelligence.
- **Stronger Solutions**: Collaborative efforts result in more comprehensive and well-thought-out solutions, as team members contribute their insights and perspectives.
- **Enhanced Problem-Solving**: Collaboration enables teams to pool their problem-solving abilities, making it easier to tackle complex challenges.
- **Effective Decision-Making**: Collaborative decision-making benefits from diverse viewpoints, leading to well-rounded and informed choices.
- **Conflict Resolution**: Leaders who encourage collaboration facilitate open discussions, leading to constructive conflict resolution and better outcomes.
- **Team Building**: Collaboration promotes a sense of camaraderie and unity among team members, strengthening team dynamics and morale.

- **Feedback Loop**: Leaders who foster collaboration create an environment where feedback flows freely, allowing team members to learn and improve.
- **Effective Communication**: Collaboration encourages open and transparent communication, ensuring that information is shared accurately and timely.
- **Effective Resource Utilization**: Collaborative efforts optimize the use of resources by tapping into each team member's strengths and skills.
- **Personal and Professional Growth**: Collaboration exposes team members to new ideas and approaches, contributing to their ongoing development.
- **Stakeholder Alignment**: Collaborative efforts consider the perspectives and needs of stakeholders, leading to solutions that align with their expectations.
- **Increased Efficiency**: Collaboration streamlines workflows and minimizes duplication of effort by leveraging the skills of the entire team.
- **Project Success**: Collaboration contributes to successful project outcomes by ensuring that all team members are aligned and working toward a common goal.
- **Culture of Teamwork**: Leaders who prioritize collaboration foster a culture where teamwork is valued, leading to improved engagement and job satisfaction.

Collaboration is essential for engineering leaders to promote teamwork, innovation, and effective problem-solving within their teams. Leaders who create an environment that encourages collaboration enable their team members to leverage each other's strengths, leading to improved project outcomes, personal growth, and a positive work culture.

Continuous Learning

Continuous learning is essential for engineering leaders as it enables them to stay relevant, adapt to changes, and lead their teams effectively in a rapidly evolving field. Leaders who prioritize continuous learning set an example for their teams, foster innovation, and contribute to long-term organizational success. Here's why continuous learning is important for an engineering leader:

- **Adaptation to Technological Advancements**: Engineering is a field that constantly evolves with new technologies. Continuous learning ensures leaders stay up-to-date with the latest trends and advancements.
- **Staying Relevant**: Continuous learning prevents leaders from becoming outdated or relying on outdated practices, ensuring their skills remain relevant and valuable.
- **Innovation**: Learning about new technologies, methods, and approaches can spark innovation and inspire leaders to bring fresh ideas to their teams.
- **Problem-Solving Skills**: Continuous learning exposes leaders to various problem-solving strategies and techniques, enhancing their ability to approach challenges creatively.
- **Effective Decision-Making**: Updated knowledge enables leaders to make informed decisions based on the latest information, data, and insights.
- **Role Modeling**: Leaders who prioritize continuous learning set an example for their teams, encouraging team members to also engage in ongoing education and development.
- **Personal Growth**: Continuous learning promotes personal growth and development, contributing to leaders' confidence and leadership skills.

- **Change Management**: Leaders who continuously learn are better equipped to navigate organizational changes and guide their teams through transitions.
- **Open-Mindedness**: Learning fosters open-mindedness, enabling leaders to consider diverse viewpoints and incorporate new ideas into their leadership approach.
- **Effective Communication**: Continuous learning improves leaders' ability to communicate complex technical concepts to both technical and non-technical stakeholders.
- **Global Perspective**: Learning about international best practices and trends expands leaders' perspectives beyond their immediate environment.
- **Networking Opportunities**: Engaging in continuous learning provides opportunities for leaders to connect with peers, mentors, and experts in the field.
- **Skill Development**: Learning new skills enhances leaders' ability to contribute to various aspects of their role and the success of their team.
- **Risk Management**: Leaders who understand emerging risks and challenges can proactively manage them, minimizing potential negative impacts.
- **Long-Term Success**: Continuous learning contributes to the long-term success of both leaders and their organizations by fostering adaptability and growth.
- **Future-Proofing**: Learning equips leaders with the tools to navigate future challenges, uncertainties, and disruptions.

Continuous learning is a cornerstone of effective leadership in engineering. Leaders who prioritize learning not only enhance their own skills and knowledge but also inspire their teams, drive innovation, and ensure their organizations remain competitive and adaptable in a rapidly changing landscape.

Results-Oriented

Being results-oriented is essential for engineering leaders as it focuses their efforts on achieving tangible outcomes, meeting goals, and driving the success of projects and teams. Leaders who prioritize results create a culture of accountability, productivity, and continuous improvement within their teams. Here's why being results-oriented is important for an engineering leader:

- **Goal Achievement**: Being results-oriented ensures that leaders and their teams work toward clear and measurable objectives, leading to successful project completion.
- **Project Success**: Leaders who prioritize results contribute to the successful execution of projects, meeting deadlines, and delivering high-quality outcomes.
- **Resource Optimization**: Being results-oriented helps leaders allocate resources efficiently to achieve optimal outcomes and manage project constraints effectively.
- **Accountability**: A results-oriented approach fosters accountability as team members are aligned with achieving specific results and are responsible for their contributions.
- **Focus on Key Priorities**: Leaders who focus on results prioritize key tasks and initiatives, directing their teams' efforts toward what matters most.
- **Performance Measurement**: Being results-oriented enables leaders to measure and evaluate team performance against predefined goals, identifying areas for improvement.
- **Innovation and Problem-Solving**: Leaders who prioritize results encourage teams to find innovative solutions to challenges to ensure successful outcomes.
- **Decision-Making Alignment**: A results-oriented approach guides leaders' decision-making, ensuring choices are aligned with achieving desired outcomes.

- **Continuous Improvement**: Being results-oriented promotes a culture of continuous improvement, where teams analyze their performance and outcomes to enhance future projects.
- **Effective Communication**: Leaders who focus on results communicate goals, expectations, and progress clearly to team members, enhancing collaboration and transparency.
- **Customer Satisfaction**: Being results-oriented aims to meet or exceed customer expectations, ensuring the delivered solutions address their needs.
- **Time Management**: Prioritizing results helps leaders manage their time effectively by focusing on tasks that contribute directly to achieving objectives.
- **Leadership Development**: A results-oriented leader can guide team members in setting and achieving their own goals, fostering their growth and development.
- **Stakeholder Alignment**: Being results-oriented ensures that stakeholders are aligned with project goals and can provide the necessary support for success.
- **Organizational Impact**: Leaders who focus on results contribute to the overall impact and success of their organization by consistently achieving meaningful outcomes.
- **Personal and Team Accountability**: A results-oriented approach encourages leaders and team members to take ownership of their responsibilities and outcomes.

Being results-oriented is a fundamental trait for engineering leaders to drive the success of projects, teams, and organizations. Leaders who prioritize results create a culture of achievement, accountability, and continuous improvement, ensuring that their efforts contribute to meaningful and impactful outcomes.

Strategic Thinking

Strategic thinking is a critical skill for engineering leaders as it enables them to anticipate future challenges, make informed decisions, and guide their teams toward long-term success. Leaders who possess strategic thinking abilities are better equipped to align their actions with the organization's goals and drive impactful outcomes. Here's why strategic thinking is important for an engineering leader:

- **Alignment with Organizational Goals**: Strategic thinking allows leaders to align their team's efforts with the overall strategic objectives of the organization, ensuring everyone is working towards the same vision.
- **Long-Term Planning**: Leaders who think strategically can develop long-term plans and roadmaps that guide their teams over extended periods, ensuring sustained success.
- **Anticipating Trends**: Strategic thinkers can analyze industry trends and anticipate changes, helping their teams adapt proactively to new technologies and market shifts.
- **Risk Management**: Leaders who think strategically can identify potential risks and challenges early on, allowing them to implement mitigation strategies and minimize negative impacts.
- **Resource Allocation**: Strategic thinking enables leaders to allocate resources effectively by prioritizing initiatives that align with the organization's strategic priorities.
- **Decision-Making**: Strategic thinkers can make informed decisions based on a thorough understanding of the bigger picture and how various options align with long-term goals.
- **Innovation and Creativity**: Strategic leaders encourage innovation by considering new approaches, technologies, and methods that can contribute to the organization's success.

- **Adaptability**: Strategic thinking helps leaders adapt to changing circumstances by providing a flexible framework that guides decision-making under different conditions.
- **Effective Communication**: Leaders who think strategically can communicate complex concepts and strategies to their teams, ensuring everyone understands the goals and direction.
- **Problem-Solving**: Strategic thinkers approach challenges with a systematic and forward-looking perspective, leading to more effective and innovative problem-solving.
- **Opportunity Recognition**: Strategic thinkers can identify and capitalize on opportunities that align with the organization's goals, leading to growth and competitive advantage.
- **Leadership Development**: Leaders who think strategically can guide their team members' professional development in alignment with the organization's future needs.
- **Team Alignment**: Strategic thinking ensures that team members are aligned with the organization's long-term vision, fostering a sense of purpose and direction.
- **Financial Management**: Leaders who think strategically make well-informed financial decisions that support the organization's growth and sustainability.
- **Balancing Short-Term and Long-Term Goals**: Strategic thinkers strike a balance between short-term deliverables and long-term objectives, ensuring that short-term wins contribute to the organization's broader success.
- **Driving Change**: Strategic leaders can lead their teams through organizational changes by articulating a clear vision and guiding steps toward achieving it.

Strategic thinking is a fundamental skill for engineering leaders to lead their teams effectively, drive innovation, and ensure the long-term success of their projects and organizations. Leaders who possess strategic thinking abilities can navigate complexities, make informed decisions, and create a roadmap for their teams to achieve meaningful and impactful results.

Feedback and Improvement

Feedback and continuous improvement are vital for engineering leaders as they enable personal growth, enhance team performance, and drive the success of projects. Leaders who prioritize feedback create a culture of open communication, learning, and innovation, fostering an environment where both individuals and teams can thrive. Here's why feedback and improvement are important for an engineering leader:

- Personal Growth: Feedback provides leaders with insights into their strengths and areas for improvement, supporting their ongoing development as effective leaders.
- Skill Enhancement: Feedback helps leaders identify gaps in their skills and knowledge, enabling them to focus on areas that will benefit their leadership capabilities.
- Self-Awareness: Regular feedback enhances leaders' self-awareness, allowing them to understand how their actions and decisions impact their team and the organization.
- Effective Communication: Leaders who encourage feedback can communicate more effectively, as they learn to tailor their messages to different audiences and respond to their needs.
- Team Performance: Constructive feedback helps leaders identify ways to support their teams better, improving performance and achieving higher levels of collaboration.
- Motivation: Leaders who provide feedback recognize and acknowledge their team members' efforts, motivating them to continue performing at their best.
- Conflict Resolution: Feedback supports conflict resolution by addressing misunderstandings or tensions early, preventing issues from escalating.

- Innovation: A culture of feedback encourages team members to share ideas and suggestions, fostering an environment of innovation and continuous improvement.
- Trust Building: Leaders who value feedback build trust with their teams by actively seeking input and demonstrating a willingness to listen and make changes.
- Performance Alignment: Feedback helps leaders ensure that their team's performance aligns with organizational goals and expectations.
- Coaching and Mentoring: Feedback allows leaders to provide coaching and mentorship tailored to individual team members' needs and aspirations.
- Problem-Solving: Leaders who receive feedback can identify recurring issues and address root causes, contributing to more effective problem-solving.
- Learning Culture: Leaders who prioritize feedback create a learning culture within their teams, promoting ongoing skill development and knowledge sharing.
- Empowerment: Constructive feedback empowers team members to take ownership of their performance and contribute to the team's success.
- Data-Informed Decisions: Feedback provides data that leaders can use to make informed decisions that benefit both their teams and the organization.
- Organizational Success: Feedback-driven improvement initiatives contribute to the overall success and effectiveness of the organization.

Feedback and continuous improvement are crucial for engineering leaders to enhance their own abilities, drive team performance, and achieve project success. Leaders who value feedback create a culture of growth and collaboration, leading to increased motivation, innovation, and long-term organizational prosperity.

Conclusion

In the ever-evolving landscape of engineering, leadership emerges as a cornerstone of success, serving as the guiding force that transforms projects, teams, and organizations. This journey through the pages of this book has explored the multifaceted role of an engineering leader, delving into the intricate balance of technical prowess, interpersonal skills, and strategic vision. As we reach the final chapter, let us reflect on the key lessons that have illuminated the path to effective engineering leadership.

The pages of this book have revealed that the essence of leadership lies not only in technical proficiency, but also in the ability to inspire, communicate, and collaborate. From the inception of a project to its final execution, an engineering leader is the beacon that navigates challenges, makes informed decisions, and empowers their team to achieve remarkable outcomes. This journey has emphasized that the true measure of leadership is not found solely in the accomplishments achieved, but in the growth and development fostered within each team member.

In the pursuit of engineering excellence, we have witnessed the transformative power of empathy, adaptability, and continuous learning. The pages have echoed with the voices of seasoned leaders who emphasize the importance of mentorship, coaching, and the delicate art of balancing results with the well-being of those under one's guidance. The stories shared have illuminated the impact of a leader's resilience in the face of adversity, and the unwavering commitment to ethical conduct that stands as the foundation of trust.

As we close this chapter, let us embrace the lessons learned and the insights gained. The role of an engineering leader is not confined to a title; it is a commitment to inspire, innovate, and elevate those who follow. It is a journey that requires a constant pursuit of self-improvement, a dedication to understanding the unique needs of one's team, and a vision that extends far beyond the immediate horizon.

May this book serve as a compass for aspiring and seasoned engineering leaders alike, reminding us that the path to success is forged not only by technical expertise, but by the unwavering dedication to guide, mentor, and inspire. As the story of engineering leadership continues to unfold, may each reader find themselves equipped with the wisdom and tools to illuminate their own unique path toward becoming exceptional leaders in the realm of engineering and beyond.